The Lighthouse Keeper's Catastrophe

Ronda & David Armitage

First published in 1986 by Scholastic Ltd
This edition first published in 2008 by Scholastic Children's Books
Euston House, 24 Eversholt Street
London NW1 1DB
a division of Scholastic Ltd
www.scholastic.co.uk
London ~ New York ~ Toronto ~ Sydney ~ Auckland
Mexico City ~ New Delhi ~ Hong Kong

Text copyright © 1986 Ronda Armitage
Illustrations copyright © 1986 David Armitage

ISBN 978 1407 10650 2

1 3 5 7 9 10 8 6 4 2

The Lighthouse Keeper's Catastrophe

Ronda & David Armitage

Mr Grinling was a lighthouse keeper. He lived with Mrs Grinling in a little white cottage on the cliffs. Every morning he rowed out to his lighthouse to clean and polish the light. Every morning Mrs Grinling prepared a delicious lunch for him.

At lunch time Mrs Grinling packed the
lunch in a basket and sent it down the wire
to the lighthouse.

On high days and holidays when the sun shone Mr and Mrs Grinling opened up the lighthouse, hung the key safely on its hook inside and spent many contented hours fishing. Hamish the cat lazed about in the sun. From time to time he roused himself to chase the seagulls. This particular morning chasing seagulls was not what Hamish had in mind. He was much too busy enjoying himself in other ways.

Mr Grinling was not at all pleased when he saw what Hamish was doing.

"Move it, pussy cat," he snarled as he chased Hamish into the lighthouse.

SLAM!!!

"That'll teach you to steal our fish, you little varmint," and without thinking he slammed the door shut.

Mr and Mrs Grinling continued with their fishing. Soon, Mr Grinling's stomach reminded him that lunch would be very welcome. As he went to let Hamish out he was struck by a terrible thought. The key, where was the lighthouse door key? Of course, it was inside.

Mr Grinling did his very best to get Hamish out of the lighthouse.

He rattled the lock as hard as he could . . .

he pushed,

he kicked . . .

. . . and he cursed

but the door stayed firmly shut.

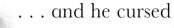

"Don't worry," soothed Mrs Grinling, "Hamish is quite safe where he is. We have the spare key in the old teapot on the mantelpiece in the kitchen."

The spare key was exactly where Mrs Grinling said it would be – in the teapot. While she prepared cold chicken sandwiches, a fruit salad with lots of strawberries and a chocolate milkshake for his lunch, Mr Grinling listened to the midday weather forecast. It was perfectly dreadful. Wind and rain with possible thunder and lightning later in the day.

"I don't like the sound of that weather, Mrs G," said Mr Grinling. "The sooner I get back to the lighthouse, rescue Hamish and switch on the light, the happier I shall be. If you could pack the lunch in the basket I'll take it with me. Remind me to take a screwdriver, Mrs G, I have some repair work to do."

So Mr Grinling set off down the steep, winding path with
his lunch and the key in the lunch basket. It was not until
he was halfway down the hill that he heard Mrs Grinling
calling from the little white cottage.
"The screwdriver, Mr G, you've
forgotten the screwdriver."

"Botheration," he muttered. Climbing cliff paths for a plump lighthouse keeper was rather hard work. He put the lunch basket on the bank and stomped back towards the house.

Oh, what a silly man, he really ought to have known better.
Already the seagulls were beginning to gather.
As he turned the corner . . .

down
they
swooped.

Such greedy creatures.
They squabbled
and flapped
and squawked
and tugged,
trying to get
to the lunch.

Finally the basket started
to move. Down the slope it went,
tumbling, bumping,

faster and faster,

over

and over

and over
until it came to the cliff edge.
For a moment it almost seemed to stop
and then . . .

it was gone.

And so was the key! Down it drifted, down past the eagle ray and the angel fish to the seabed. There it lay amongst the rocks and the seaweed where only the octopus, the crab and other sea creatures would ever find it again.

Mr Grinling was very puzzled upon his return. It was not until Mrs Grinling came to help him search that she found the bits of cold chicken and the odd strawberry. But no lighthouse key – not on the slope – not anywhere.

"Oh, you are a foolish man, Mr G," she exclaimed. "All your life you've lived amongst seagulls and still you leave your lunch for them to eat."

Mr Grinling smiled rather foolishly. "I'm sure we have a third key somewhere." Mrs Grinling shook her head, "I don't think so," she said. "Don't you remember, one dropped through the hole in your trousers last year."

Already the sky was beginning to fill with clouds. "Well, there's nothing for it, Mr G," said Mrs Grinling. "You'll just have to climb in." So they collected the ladder and rowed back to the lighthouse.

While Mrs Grinling held the ladder Mr Grinling climbed very slowly to the top. "I don't like this, Mrs G," he called, "you know I get dizzy when I climb up high." "Don't look down," she replied, "think of Hamish, think of the light, think of all those poor ships that might be wrecked unless that light shines tonight." But in the end it was not dizziness that stopped Mr Grinling.

Oh, dearie me, no. It was all those scrumptious lunches he had eaten. In through the window he climbed and there he stuck fast. Neither backwards nor forwards could he go – he was just too fat.

Nor could Mrs Grinling help him. She pushed and she pulled and pulled and pushed until he squealed but she couldn't get him to move.

"I'm sorry, Mr G," she said, "there's only one thing to be done – I'll have to remove those great heavy trousers."

Off came the boots and off came the trousers. Mr Grinling wriggled again and at last he was free.

Rowing home was difficult for Mr and Mrs Grinling.
The wind was almost gale force by now
and the waves kept breaking over the
bow of the little boat.

Cottage door keys (front)

"There must be another key somewhere," said Mr Grinling, "we'll just have to search until we find it." And search they did. They opened old tins and jars, they emptied out drawers and they peered into cupboards but to no avail – no key labelled LIGHTHOUSE could be found.

Old key from a wrecked ship

Cottage door key (back)

Toolshed key

Red Suitcase key

First-aid box key

Blue Suitcase key

Weather station key

"I'll just have to cycle into the village and alert the coastguards," said Mr Grinling.

"No time," said Mrs Grinling. "Look at that sky. You'll never get there before dark and you haven't got a light on your bike. But I've got an idea – a perfectly brilliant idea."

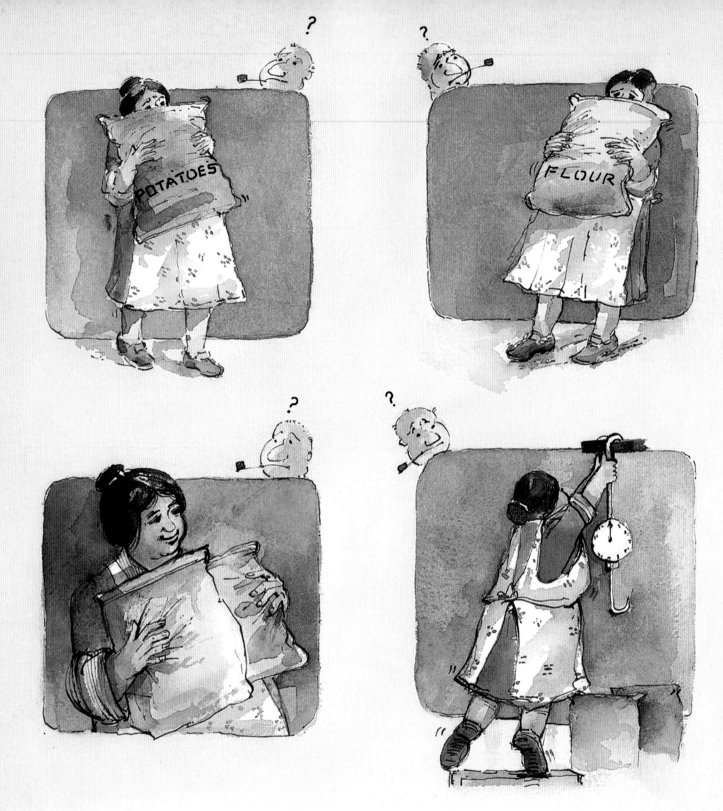

While Mr Grinling looked on Mrs Grinling rushed about the little white cottage gathering up all manner of things. She put everything she had collected into a large sack.

She weighed the sack and then she weighed Mr Grinling. Mr Grinling began to feel nervous but he wasn't quite sure why.

?

By the time Mrs Grinling had attached the sack to the pulley and sent it down the wire, Mr Grinling was biting his fingernails and muttering to himself.

Mrs Grinling smiled happily. "That worked perfectly," she said. "Your turn now."

Mr Grinling's legs became quite wobbly and he had to sit down quickly in the chair. "Me," he squeaked, "on that wire – all the way to the lighthouse? You know I am terrified of thunder and lightning, Mrs Grinling – how could you suggest such an idea on a night like this?"

Mrs Grinling spoke to him in a stern voice. "You must be brave, Mr Grinling, think of your poor little Hamish all alone in the dark. Think of all the ships that might be lost because your light isn't shining."

Mr Grinling shuddered. "Of course you're quite right, Mrs Grinling, I must be brave. I am the lighthouse keeper and come rain or shine I must tend that light."

Without further ado, Mr Grinling climbed into
his wet weather gear, fastened the harness
around himself and attached it to the pulley.
A quick glance back at his comfortable
armchair, a big kiss of luck from Mrs Grinling,
and out he swung into the dark, wet night.

HAMISH

Mrs Grinling watched until Mr Grinling became a tiny speck in the darkness. The minutes ticked by and nothing happened. Mrs Grinling became quite agitated; why was it taking so long? Had something happened to Mr Grinling?

At last she was able to uncross her fingers and smile again. Her plan had worked. Mr Grinling and Hamish were safe. For there it was for all the ships to see – the light shining steadily and bravely across the ocean.